Original title:
Freeze! You're Under a Snowstorm

Copyright © 2024 Creative Arts Management OÜ
All rights reserved.

Author: Gideon Barrett
ISBN HARDBACK: 978-9916-94-316-8
ISBN PAPERBACK: 978-9916-94-317-5

The Frosty Veil of Eternity

The snowflakes swirl with glee,
As I stumble, oh dear me!
My nose is red, and hair's a fright,
Adventures in the snowy night.

A penguin slides, and so do I,
We both take off, oh my, oh my!
Chasing snowballs, dodging trees,
What is this, a winter tease?

I built a man, but he can't stand,
He's tipping over, isn't it grand?
With buttons for eyes and a carrot nose,
He waves goodbye as he slowly goes.

Hot cocoa waits, a cozy treat,
Melting marshmallows, oh-so-sweet.
Laughter echoes, joy in the air,
In this chilly land, without a care.

Between the Snowy Boundaries

In the air, a flurry prances,
Snowflakes dancing, doing chances.
In my boots, I squeeze a sneeze,
Hats are worn like funny peas.

Slip and slide, oh what a thrill,
Neighbors' snowmen need a fill.
One has a carrot for a nose,
But I swear it winked, who knows?

Remnants of a Whirling Chill

Chasing shadows, I'm a spy,
Stealthy behind the snowy pie.
Look at me, I'm quite the sight,
Wobbly waddling, oh so bright.

A snowball battles, oh what fun,
Direct hit—who threw that one?
Laughter echoes through the cold,
Around the drifts, my friends I hold.

Heartbeats in a Snow-Swept Realm

Snowflakes tickle, then they tease,
Catching cheeks with chilly breeze.
I lost my mitten to the fluff,
My hands are cold, but that's enough!

In the frosty, crisp delight,
Snowballs fuse like a lovers' fight.
Rolling, tumbling, joy complete,
On this white and wobbly seat.

The Legend of the Stillness

In the stillness, whispers play,
Giggling children pass the day.
Once a tree sprouted a hat,
Claimed a squirrel—how about that?

Pinecones chuckle on the ground,
While we frolic all around.
Magic's found in every flake,
A giggle here, a funny quake.

Flakes of Silence

White confetti fills the air,
As penguins prance without a care.
Snowflakes tickle noses bright,
While squirrels slip, oh what a sight!

Hot cocoa spills, oh what a mess,
Frothy mustaches, I confess.
Snowmen wobble, hats askew,
A snowball flies! Missed you too!

The Frost's Embrace

Icicles dangle, dripping slow,
Like icy dancers, putting on a show.
Frosty friends in winter's cheer,
With giggles loud, we persevere.

A frozen rubber chicken flies,
Landing soft beneath the skies.
Laughter echoes, pure delight,
As snowflakes twirl in space tonight!

Shivering Shadows

Footprints lead where snowflakes fall,
But some are tiny, some are tall.
A snowball fight begins to brew,
With targets set—oh wait, is that you?

Giggles and shouts fill the night,
As snowmen stumble, oh what a sight!
With scarves wrapped tight around our necks,
We tease the frosty likes of Rex!

A Dance of Icicles

Icicles sway, a frozen jig,
While winter winds dance, oh so big.
Chattering teeth and drippy noses,
As snowflakes land on winter poses.

Candy canes stick on a tree,
But sweet snowflakes—such a spree!
In this chaos of winter fun,
Who knew a snowstorm could weigh a ton?

A Blanket of Cold

A chilly chill begins to creep,
Soft flakes fall, not a peep.
Socks are wet, shoes are gone,
Who's that sneezing? Oh, come on!

Snowmen form without much haste,
Lumpy bodies, funny-faced.
Where's my scarf? I need a glove!
Oh wait, that's the cat I love!

Whirling Wonders

Round and round, a flurry twirls,
A dance of cold, and hair it curls.
Children laugh, a snowball flies,
My face—it's now a snowy disguise!

Chasing friends, we tumble down,
Snowflakes stuck on all around.
Whoops! A slip, a fumble, a fall,
Nothing better—just snow and brawl!

Glistening Ruins

In the yard, a castle stands,
With frozen flags and snowy bands.
But look, a cat climbs to the top,
And down it goes with one big plop!

Glittering piles, a sparkling mess,
A place for fun, but not for stress.
What a sight, the chaos grows,
As down we tumble, in frozen clothes!

Veil of Snow

Drifting down, a soft white shroud,
Whispers giggles, beneath a cloud.
Snowflakes tickle, oh what glee!
I can't catch them—they're too free!

In this world, we leap and dart,
With icy flair and chilly heart.
But watch your step, or you might find,
Icy puddles! Oh, never mind!

The Stillness Before

In the hush of the morning, cats in rows,
Snowflakes tumble where cold wind blows.
Pajamas bundled, we sip our tea,
While flakes dance around like they're wild and free.

Sleds wait patiently at the door,
Hats and mittens drop on the floor.
The street's a canvas, all blank and white,
Just waiting for chaos to take flight.

Glacial Reverie

Two snowmen chat with carrot noses,
Trading tales of warm sun poses.
A snowball fight breaks out with glee,
Oops! Right in the face! - Oh, woe is me!

With each slip and slide we all proclaim,
Winter's a party, never the same.
The dog rolls by, a furry cheerleader,
While we all cheer, 'Go, flurry, go faster!'

Tempest Beneath the Tundra

Wind whoops and howls, it's quite a plot,
The cat dives under the couch, what a spot!
Neighbors holler over piles of snow,
With cheeks like cherries, the laughter will flow.

Icicles dangle like teeth from above,
Children throw snowballs, all in good love.
Hot cocoa steams, marshmallows afloat,
Just keep the mittens dry, that's the note!

An Aerial Embrace

Flurries whirl like they're in disguise,
Snowflakes giggle as they cloud our skies.
A collision of hats, a splash of white,
Each merry laugh, a pure delight!

From rooftops to sidewalks, a bed so grand,
We trudge through drifts, snowmen hand in hand.
With cheeks so rosy and spirits bright,
We dance through the chaos, oh, what a sight!

Dances with the Drifts

The snowflakes twirl, what a sight,
Spinning around in the pale moonlight.
Penguins in mittens, they flop and slide,
Winter's a party, come join the ride!

Snowmen wobble with carrot noses,
Shaking their hips, striking silly poses.
A snowball fight breaks out in glee,
Who knew winter could be so free?

Sleds flying high, laughter so bright,
In a world where everything's white.
We dance through drifts, no care for the chill,
In this frosty playground, we laugh at will!

Frost-Bitten Memories

Remember the time when we slipped on ice?
Landed in snow, didn't think twice!
Our faces adorned with bright white fluff,
Winter's sweet grip is just silly enough.

Hot cocoa spills from our tiny cups,
As we tumble like goofballs, tripping up.
Snowflakes in noses, giggles galore,
Who knew winter could equal such lore?

Warmed by the fire, we tell the tales,
Of frosty escapades and snowy trails.
Memories twinkling, brighter than light,
In this frozen wonder, everything's right!

In the Heart of the Storm

Whirling chaos, oh what a blend,
As snowflakes fight, it's hard to pretend.
I go left, and you dash right,
Winter's a circus, what a delight!

Socks on our hands, we build with glee,
Lopsided snowballs, come roll with me.
But wait, what's that? A snowman collides!
He's tipped over, but joy still abides!

Around and around, we stumble and trip,
Hoisted by laughter, oh what a slip!
In twinkling weather, our spirits conform,
What fun we seek in the heart of the storm!

Snowbound Whispers

Through whispered winds, the snowflakes tease,
We land in piles, like leaves on trees.
Bundle up tight, here comes the chill,
But inside our laughter can warm up a hill!

The cat's in a hat, a scarf on his paw,
Chasing the flakes, oh, what a flaw!
He pounces and tumbles, a furry ball,
In this snowy wonderland, we all have a ball!

With snow-covered rooftops and giggles that weave,
Whispers of winter, let's not leave.
In drifts and snowbanks, our hearts will race,
In winter's embrace, we find our place!

Dreams on Ice

Skating on dreams with a crunch and a splash,
The frosty flakes fall, making quite the bash.
A penguin in mittens joins in on the fun,
Slipping and sliding, oh what a run!

Snowmen are laughing, their buttons askew,
Toboggans are racing, through snowdrifts they flew.
With snowballs like missiles, they fly through the air,
Who knew winter's chaos could be such a flair!

The Whispering White

The snowflakes whisper in giggles and cheer,
They flutter like whispers, so light and dear.
A bunny in boots hops around all aglow,
Waving at snowflakes that jive to and fro.

A snow angel flails in a flurry so bright,
With wings made of snow that take off in flight.
Chilly confetti, a wild, wacky show,
Who knew such a storm could invite quite the row!

A Symphony of Sleet

A clang and a clatter, the wind starts to sing,
As ice-cold percussion makes jingle bells ring.
The rooftops are drumming with flurries that fall,
While snowmen audition for the grandest of balls.

The boots tap a rhythm on sidewalks aglow,
As laughter erupts in a twinkling snow.
Hot cocoa's the encore, a treat to enjoy,
In this winter concert, oh what a joy!

Bound in Snow

Caught in a blanket so fluffy and white,
The ground is now giggling, what a silly sight!
A squirrel in a scarf tries to find his lost acorn,
While snowflakes are tickling, a storm to adorn.

Frosty the jester prances with glee,
He slips, he spins, just to be free.
Snowdrifts are mountains, a playground to share,
In this whimsical world, all worries clear as air!

Shattered Winter's Embrace

Icicles dangle from my nose,
I thought I'd make some snowman toes.
But slipped and fell in powdery fluff,
Now I'm stuck like an oversized muff.

Snowflakes tumble like playful sprites,
Waltzing down in swirling flights.
I threw a snowball, hit my dog,
He thinks it's just a frosty fog.

My mittens are soaked, my toes are cold,
Winter's charm is getting old.
But there's hot cocoa waiting near,
Time to toast the snowy cheer!

Old man Winter, what a clown,
Turns the town into a white gown.
With each soft flake, my laughter grows,
In this silly snowy show, who knows?

A Tapestry in White

The world is wrapped in fluffy sheets,
Nature's quilt of snowy treats.
But as I stroll on winter's stage,
I swear, I've seen snowmen rage!

Sledding down the hill with glee,
I wobbled and yelled, "Look at me!"
But face-first was my final call,
Now my face is a snowball.

With every gust my hat takes flight,
Chasing it brings endless delight.
It danced away, such a cheeky brat,
I'm in a chase with a furry cat!

Snow angels wave, but they can't fly,
They giggle at my frigid sigh.
In this frosty, funny show,
Winter's antics steal the show!

Specters of the Snowbound Night

Night descends with a snowy blanket,
The moon peeks out, who'll prank it?
I swear I saw a snowman grin,
With a carrot nose, a goofy kin!

A walking snowdrift just strolled by,
Tipped its hat and waved, oh my!
Caught in laughter, a blizzard song,
Who knew snow could be so wrong?

Snowball fights that leave you sore,
Yet I can't help but ask for more.
Laughter bubbling like hot soup,
As I slip into the frosty loop!

With snowflakes dancing on my nose,
I smile wide as winter glows.
In this chilly night of play,
I'll dance until the dawn's first ray!

When the World Bows to Ice

Icebergs form in my backyard,
My dog slides past, he's gone too far!
I tried to skate, but lost my flair,
Now I'm just a statue there!

All the kids scream with delight,
As they whip past me, quite a sight!
I'm helpless on this icy slide,
An unintended wobbly ride!

Snowballs launch like cannonballs,
My best friend hides behind the walls.
But I pelt him with such grace,
We laugh until we can't keep pace!

The world adorned in winter's veil,
Together we could tell a tale.
In this icy twist and play,
We'll sled into a snowy day!

Snowflakes and Sighs

Little flakes drop from the sky,
Dancing like they want to fly.
Hats askew, scarves wrapped tight,
Noses red, oh what a sight!

Snowballs flying through the air,
Someone lands without a care.
Giggles echo, laughter rings,
Winter joy, oh what it brings!

Slipping, sliding, whoops, a tumble,
Watch me now as I stumble!
Hot cocoa waits, a sweet warm treat,
After all this snowy feat!

Mittens lost, chilled fingers bare,
Frozen cheeks, but who would care?
In the flurry, smiles abound,
Find the joy in snowy ground!

The Dance of Frozen Ferns

Ferns adorned in frosty lace,
Wobbling, shaking, what a place!
Wind whispers secrets, soft and low,
Here comes the fun, let's start the show!

We twirl and spin, what a sight!
Ready for mischief, hearts so light.
But oh no! A slip, a slide,
Laughter bursts with every glide!

Snowflakes bounce on frozen leaves,
Nature's giggle, oh how it weaves.
Frosty patterns, artists bright,
Every angle, pure delight!

With happy feet in winter cheer,
Join the dance, bring the cheer!
Slip and trip, it's quite a scene,
In this snowy art routine!

Eyes Frozen in Wonder

Look at those tumbling winds,
Pulling us into winter spins.
Cheeks are rosy, breath like steam,
It's a chilly, frosty dream!

Snowflakes gather, a cozy mix,
Wandering through the frosty fix.
With every step, a crunch so loud,
Jokes are made to share with the crowd!

Snowmen sporting hats askew,
Waving hello as we pass through.
Snowball fights, a playful clash,
Mirth and giggles, then a splash!

But beware those stealthy tricks,
From that tree branch, snowy flicks!
Eyes wide open, laughter flows,
Joyful hearts in winter's toes!

Twilight of the Tundra

At dusk, the snow begins to glow,
The world wrapped up in frosty flow.
Furry boots and blankets tight,
Waddle onward, oh what a sight!

Snowflakes twinkle like tiny stars,
As we adventure near and far.
Life is rough, but oh so sweet,
With fluffy pillows 'neath our feet!

Watch your step on icy feet,
Or take a tumble, that's the feat!
Snow banks calling, a fort to make,
This winter bliss, for fun's own sake!

So gather close, share a grin,
For the snowy joys we find within.
As twilight falls, let laughter ring,
In the kingdom of winter, we are kings!

Beneath a Canopy of Flurries

Look up, the flakes are twirling fast,
A dance of white, they've come to last.
They tickle cheeks and melt on tongues,
Like candy falling from the lungs.

Snowmen grinning with carrot noses,
They wave at me, like silly poses.
With limbs of sticks and hats of wood,
I laugh and stomp; it feels so good.

Penguins sliding down the hill,
In coats of fluff, they thrill and chill.
Sleds zoom past in a snowy blur,
While laughter echoes with each purr.

So gather 'round, let's make a cheer,
For snowy days are full of cheer.
We'll build a fort and throw some balls,
In this white wonderland, we all enthrall.

Frostbitten Fantasies

A snowflake lands upon my hat,
It tickles me—imagine that!
I swat it off, but more do land,
A winter party made unplanned.

Socks pulled up, and mittens tight,
I waddle out, a comical sight.
The ground a canvas of pure delight,
My clumsy dance brings pure insight.

Icicles hanging like giant spears,
I swing and dodge while fighting fears.
Each step I take is a cautious mess,
Oh, winter joy, you are my dress!

With cocoa warm and marshmallows float,
My heart is light, I sing and gloat.
A snowball fight ensues with glee,
These frostbitten dreams just make me free.

Enchanted by the Drift

Underneath the fluffy veil,
My boots leave tracks like brazen trails.
I twirl around, a carefree sprite,
While snowflakes join the festive flight.

The ground is soft, a pillow white,
I launch my self with all my might.
A belly flop, I glide and slide,
In this wintry world, I take great pride.

The branches groan, they bend and sway,
A winter symphony at play.
With snowmen laughing, drinks in hand,
I join the circus—how grand, how grand!

So here I am, in pure delight,
With frosty kisses on my slight.
In snowdrifts deep, my heart takes wing,
Beautiful chaos, let joy take spring!

Secrets of a Snow-Laden Silence

The world grows hushed beneath the snow,
A winter blanket, soft and slow.
Every step is a crunching sound,
Like laughter echoing all around.

Snowflakes whisper secrets sweet,
As I dance and tap my frozen feet.
In quietude, the magic swells,
With tales that only snow can tell.

Mittens mismatched, my nose turned red,
I tumble down, thoughts in my head.
Red cheeks frolic in snowy bliss,
Every chill is a cozy kiss.

So raise a mug and toast the chill,
With laughter, joy, and snowy thrill.
In winter's grasp, let's play and sing,
For peace and fun—the joy they bring!

The Starlit Winter's Cloak

Snowflakes dance like little sprites,
Frosty noses, chilly sights.
Sleds parade down icy lanes,
With laughter echoing like trains.

Hot cocoa spills, a marshmallow dive,
Winter's here, let's all jive!
But wait, what's that? Oh my stars!
The snowman wore my old guitars!

Socks that slip and mittens lost,
Ice-cream cones at frosty cost.
But every tumble, every cheer,
Makes winter's frolic oh so dear!

So bundle up, it's time to play,
In this blanket, come what may.
Underneath this twinkling dome,
We find ourselves, we feel at home.

Shadows in the Snowfall

Sneaky shadows prance around,
Under blankets, they are found.
A snowball here, a cup of cheer,
Winter whispers, "Meet me near!"

Footprints lead to nowhere fast,
Mittens vanish; guess I'll bask.
Frigid winds will steal my hat,
Oh, how I wish for a warm flat!

Neighbors chuckling, with frosted hair,
Lost my scarf amongst the flares.
Laughter mingles with the snow,
Who knew being chilly could steal the show?

Well, if we shiver and we grin,
Let's twirl and let the fun begin!
Grab your sleds; let's make a scene,
In this snowy frolic, we're all keen!

Crystal Veils of the Night

Stars twinkle through the snowy veil,
With icy breezes that tell a tale.
Sleds zoom past with giggles bright,
As shadows leap into the night.

Chasing snowflakes, dodging cold,
Hot chocolate stories we have told.
But uh-oh! What's on my nose?
A snowball's thrown—well, who knows?

Building forts with topsy towers,
Frosted battles for hours and hours.
Yet, slipping here and stumbling there,
Makes every fall an act of flair!

Woolen capers and frosty feet,
In this wonderland, all's sweet.
So join the dance beneath the light,
In winter's gown, all feels so right!

Frost's Gentle Command

Under a blanket of softest snow,
Where winter whispers, 'Let's take it slow.'
A snowflake pops; we give a cheer,
Crisp air buzzing with holiday cheer!

Look at that fellow, stuck in a tree,
What do you mean? He's not like me!
With frosty antics all around,
The icy fun knows no bound!

Snowmen waddle, arms askew,
"Please don't sit; it's not for you!"
Careful now, with cheeks aglow,
Slipping on ice, it's quite a show!

So gather 'round and bring a smile,
For winter's joy is worth the while.
Through sparkling nights and frosty days,
Let's dance about in snow-filled ways!

Winter's Whispering Veil

Puffing out cheeks, we march with glee,
A flurry of snowflakes dance on spree.
Laughter erupts with each chilly tumble,
That snowman's scarf? Oh, what a jumble!

Branches adorned with a blanket of white,
It's hard to see straight in pure frosty light.
Hot cocoa spills from our laughing mugs,
As we slip and slide, giving each other shrugs!

Shapes of the Shivering

Outside the window, the world's gone awry,
A snowball fight breaks out—oh my, oh my!
We shape tiny snowmen with buttons for eyes,
But they tip and tumble—what a surprise!

The dog pounces in, creating a mess,
A snowdrift monster—we can only guess.
With every slip, there's a shout and a grin,
This winter's breeze will never wear thin!

The Frozen Horizon

Gazing afar at the snow-covered trees,
A squirrel slides down with a flair that'd please.
Giggling kids with cheeks bright and red,
They tumble and roll; oh, the fun we've bred!

As icicles dangle like teeth from the eaves,
Our snow fort's a fortress—where everyone believes.
But one little jab sends our hero to fall,
"Rescue me, quick!" echoes through the squall!

Echoes of the Icelands

Up on the hill, with a sled made of dreams,
We zoom down the slope, hear the laughter's gleams.
But somehow we spin, and I swear I might fly,
Past a snowman who's wearing a very strange tie!

Chasing after snowflakes, they giggle away,
While all our warm gloves go missing at play.
Hot chocolate's aroma fills the snowy air,
But we're slipping on ice—who cares? We don't care!

Chill of the Whispering Winds

A snowman wobbles on a peg,
He's made of coffee, not a leg.
His carrot nose is quite the sight,
He slips and slides, oh what a fright!

The frosty flakes dance in midair,
Socks on hands, oh what a pair.
The dog does zoomies through the snow,
While children giggle, 'Look at Joe!'

Chill divides the hot cocoa's fate,
As marshmallows float and congregate.
A snowball fight, a sly retreat,
Who's the target? No one, sweet!

And as we trudge back to our homes,
In icicles, a penguin roams.
This winter mischief, joy and cheer,
We'll brave the storm with laughter near.

Elysium of Frosted Dreams

In snowsuits thick, we tumble down,
Making snow angels, giggles abound.
Hot chocolate spills, oh what a mess,
An artist gone wrong in snowstorm stress!

A penguin slide, we fashion forth,
Running on snow, our ha-ha worth.
Beards of frost and lashes freeze,
Chasing snowflakes, what a tease!

With snowflakes twirling, here they twirled,
A carousel spun by our wild world.
Laughter erupts as we all fall,
Into white fluff, our snowball brawl!

Each frosty phase brings joy immense,
Snowball counters, a simple defense.
Elysium found in chill's embrace,
We'll meet the storm with a funny face!

The Tempest's Icy Grasp

Winds howl like a playful hound,
As snowflakes pirouette around.
The frostbite's joke? It's a prank,
When mittens vanish in the bank!

Under the storm, with flurries near,
We gear up, giggling without fear.
Slipping on ice, oh what a dance,
Getting back up? Not a chance!

Sledding down hills with squeaky cheer,
A frosty face grips, never fear.
The snow plow roars, a pop-up show,
Let's build a fort, who will throw?

With hot cider sold on the street,
Spilling it fast, what a retreat!
In the grasp of winter's charm,
Laughter reigns, we all stay warm!

Blizzards of the Heart

The sky's a swirl of white and fun,
With snowflakes dancing, everyone.
We bundle tight in hats and gloves,
Making legends of winter loves!

A snowball zooms, a daring feat,
In park lanes, our frosty seat.
With cheeks aglow and noses bright,
Yelling 'You're it!' in pure delight!

A snow-covered world, a fluffy pillow,
Under every tree, dance with the willow.
In blizzards' joy, we're silly sprites,
Painting smiles in frosty bites!

We twirl beneath the snowy haze,
As laughter echoes in snowy bays.
With snowflakes' charm, so light and free,
Our hearts are warm in winter's spree!

Ghostly White

I stepped outside with glee and cheer,
But the snowflakes laughed, I jumped in fear.
A ghostly blanket, soft and bright,
The chill made my nose turn pinkish-white.

My dog took off, a snowball beast,
He rolled and tumbled, thought it a feast.
I tried to follow, but slipped and fell,
Landed face-first; oh, what a spell!

The neighbors chuckled, sipping their tea,
While I grinned wide, stuck like a tree.
The snow kept piling, so much to gain,
But all I got was a frosty stain!

Next time I'll build a warm, snug fort,
With cocoa on hand, I'll find my support.
For when the drifts start to dance and twirl,
I'll make sure to stay indoors, give it a whirl!

Stormy Serenade

A blizzard's tune played loud and clear,
With snowflakes tapping on my ear.
The wind chimed in, a howling song,
As I bundled up, where did I go wrong?

With every gust, I took a step back,
It felt like fighting a winter attack.
My scarf wrapped tight, my coat a mess,
Each twirl I did was a comical press!

The trees were dancing, dressed in white,
While I was battling flakes left and right.
I twirled and spun, arms all a-flail,
Considered a penguin, starting to wail!

But laughter bubbled like hot cocoa's brew,
In this frosty scene, I found my view.
For every slip and snowy tumble,
Made my winter heart feel ever so humble!

Lost in a Flurry

Oh, where's my hat? It's gone with the breeze,
The snow is fluffy and sticks to my knees.
I squint at the ground, where are my feet?
This winter wonderland's turned into a feat!

I waved at a snowman, thought it was Tim,
But it just stared, its eyes so grim.
With a face like that, I decided to scoff,
And chuck a snowball to throw it off!

Each flake that fell was a ticket to fun,
Yet somehow, I tripped; oh dear, what a run!
I thought I was sprightly, full of cheer,
Until I landed, caught in a pile here!

So here I lay, arms and legs spread wide,
A snow angel-maker, I can't let it slide.
Lost in a flurry, covered in white,
I'll laugh at my mess, a winter delight!

Chasing the Chill

The frost nipped my toes as I laced my shoe,
With visions of snowmen, I thought I knew.
But as soon as I stepped, the world went wild,
Snowflakes flung everywhere, a blizzard beguiled!

I attempted to run, but slipped on a patch,
Teetering like a juggler, watching the match.
At the end of my chase, I gave a loud caw,
Chasing the chill, I found snow in my maw!

The world turned white, a carnival scene,
My snow-covered glasses, so very obscene.
But laughter erupted, my cheeks turned red,
Lucky for me, I'm easily fed!

With friends gathered round, we'd roll and we'd glide,
Creating a ruckus, stuck, side-by-side.
In this wintry party, one thing's for sure,
Chasing the chill means joy, I endure!

Shivering Shades of Winter

A squirrel in mittens, quite a sight,
He wobbles and tumbles, oh what a fright.
Snowballs are flying, a wild game starts,
With snow on our heads, we're all works of art.

The carriages stuck, slipping and sliding,
Like a winter ballet, no one is gliding.
Hot cocoa in hand, we sit by the fire,
Telling goofy tales, our laughter goes higher.

We stumble on ice, wearing bright scarves,
With noses so red, like we've taken a carves.
We dart to our homes, avoiding the chill,
But our hearts dance around, what a winter thrill!

Snowmen are grinning, with carrots askew,
They wear hats made from socks and an old shoe.
In this wacky wonder, we find our delight,
While the world looks like magic, oh what a sight!

Whiteout Serenade

The flakes start to tumble, a fluffy parade,
A glimpse of the world in a snowy charade.
Our boots are all soggy, shoes made for spring,
But we'll splash through the puddles and burst into sing!

Down with a thud on the slippery ground,
The laughter erupts, such joy to be found.
With hats pulled down low and mittens so tight,
We embrace the white chaos; it's pure delight!

The dog darts around in a frenzy of fun,
His antics amusing, he's second to none.
Snowflakes a-flying, they tickle our nose,
As we giggle and wiggle, so silly it goes.

From window to window, we watch all the play,
While outside the kids paint the world in a spray.
With mischief and cheer, it's the wildest scene,
This blustery dance keeps our spirits so keen!

A Dance Beneath the Snowflakes

Two kids in a circle dance round and round,
With each snowy swirl, they leap off the ground.
A jump and a twirl, then a giggle and shout,
They create a snowstorm, oh, what's it about?

The world turned a canvas, so fluffy and bright,
We make footprints that vanish by morning light.
With snowballs like cannonballs flying about,
The frosty air shimmers with sparkling shout!

In this winter wonder, we spin like mad,
Chasing each other, ever so glad.
With cheeks rosy red and laughter our theme,
A whirl in the flakes, it feels like a dream!

As night begins falling, we gather our gear,
With cold little noses, we huddle near.
To share all the stories, of battles and fun,
Then wave to the snowflakes, our day's nearly done!

The Silence of Frosted Echoes

The streets are enchanted, hush drapes like a veil,
As snowflakes settle down, they dance without fail.
We venture outside, our laughter a breeze,
In sweaters and boots, we trudge with such ease.

The air is so brisk; our breath puffs out white,
With snowmen a-watching, they grin with delight.
A face made of buttons, two lumps for a nose,
He holds up a sign that says, "Come, let it snow!"

We brazenly tumble, in heaps they all land,
Our bodies like tumbleweeds, oh isn't it grand?
With mittens all soggy and cheeks that are pink,
We laugh louder still with each clatter and clink.

As day turns to night and the stars start to peek,
We gather together, embracing the freak.
With whispers of warmth and dreams to unfold,
The quiet of winter, my heart feels so bold!

Echoes of Icy Winds

The snowflakes dance like silly fools,
Wearing tiny hats and fuzzy shoes.
They twirl around in a clumsy flight,
Making snow angels in sheer delight.

A squirrel slips on a frozen branch,
Lands in a pile—does a little prance.
It shakes its head like it's sorely vexed,
Pondering life's odd winter texts.

Hot cocoa mugs now serve as shields,
As snowballs come flying from icy fields.
With laughter ringing and cheeks all aglow,
The neighborhood turns into a comic show.

Packing down snow for a lopsided fort,
Whacking your pals is the winter sport.
In the midst of it all, there's a raucous cheer,
Who knew white fluff could bring such good beer?

Nature's Arctic Roar

The winter wind laughs with a shivery song,
Cackling at snowmen who stand far too long.
With buttons for eyes and scarves wrapped tight,
They watch from their posts, unmoving at night.

Fluffy white critters pop out with glee,
Chasing each other round every tree.
The great frosty air is their playground grand,
As snowflakes tumble like a dizzy band.

Snowballs flying like mischievous dreams,
Kids dive for cover, or so it seems.
The giggles erupt as the icy winds moan,
A wintertime circus of merriment sown.

And as the sun sets, with a rosy hue,
The laughter lingers, with each frosty view.
So let the cold come; we'll battle and play,
In this world of wonder where fun leads the way!

Shattering Silence

The hush of the snow is a quiet parade,
While snowmen plot on their ice-cube charades.
With carrot noses and stick arms they scheme,
To entertain kids in their winter dream.

A plump little penguin steals leaves for a hat,
Carelessly slipping, who's laughing at that?
The ground sparkles bright, a jester's delight,
As snowflakes tumble down from their height.

Icicles hang like teeth from the eaves,
Glistening softly, like mischief that thieves.
With an echoing pop, a snowball is thrown,
Breaking the silence—oh how it has grown!

Each flurry creates a big giggling ruckus,
As clouds stuff the sky like a chubby circus.
Laughter resounds through the frosty veneer,
What fun and chaos awaits us, oh dear!

The Winter's Tale

With puffed-out cheeks, we stumble around,
Tripping on layers of soft cotton ground.
Snow-laden branches shake lightly with mirth,
As winter unfolds a comedy's birth.

Mittens mismatched, boots two sizes too large,
We wobble and glide like a grand snowflake barge.
The snowman aside watches with glee,
As we tumble and roll, carefree as can be.

A snowball misfired, lands right on Dad,
He opens his mouth, now look at him mad!
The air fills with laughter, a glorious sound,
On this winter's stage, joy knows no bound.

So grab a warm drink, let's toast to the chill,
In all of this winter, we've had quite a thrill.
With each chuckle and cheer, let the snowstorms parade,
For life's funny tales are here to be made!

Winter's Relentless Grip

A chill creeps in, it's time to run,
Hats and mittens, oh what fun!
Slip and slide on icy ground,
Watch your step, don't fall down!

The snowflakes dance, they swirl and twirl,
Making snowmen, give them a whirl!
Snowballs fly from left to right,
Laughter echoes through the night!

Our car is stuck, wheels spin and spin,
We push and shove, then we give in.
Lost in white, where's the way home?
Someone just called for a snow dome!

So grab your cocoa, warm it hot,
In this winter wonder, we'll find a spot.
Jokes and giggles, let them flow,
In winter's grip, we steal the show!

Footprints in Frost

Tiny prints in the fresh white snow,
Follow them fast, don't move slow!
Is it a rabbit, or a big old cat?
Maybe it's just the neighbor's brat!

We trek through drifts, oh what a mess,
Each step we take, we can't help but guess.
Is that a bear or just some leaves?
It's hard to tell in the snow that weaves!

Sledding down hills, oh what a blast,
But who's that yelling? "I'm stuck! Help fast!"
Buried in snow, it's quite a sight,
We'll dig you out, just not tonight!

Footprints lead us round and round,
Towards hot chocolate, where joy is found.
In this frosty land we learn to play,
Making memories on a winter day!

The Sky's Frozen Tears

Pitter patter on the ground,
The sky is crying, what a sound!
Plop, plop, splash, oh what a mess,
Nature's game of winter chess!

Hats fly off in a swooshy gust,
Snowflakes prance, in them we trust.
I thought I saw a penguin glide,
But it was just my friend, full of pride!

The trees are heavy, all dressed in white,
Branches laden, oh what a sight!
Shake off the snow, we'll dance around,
Though the gusts make us fall to the ground!

With frosty laughter, we cheer and shout,
Let's grab our sleds and head right out.
The sky's frozen tears bring us cheer,
In this winter wonder, no need to fear!

Hushed by the Blizzard

Whispers hush through the snowy night,
Like a blanket, it feels so right.
But wait, what's that? A loud crunch sound,
Oh no, it's snow tires spinning round!

Snowflakes tumble, swirling down,
They settle softly without a frown.
Sleds whoosh by with giggles galore,
Digging out the neighbor from their door!

A snowman needs a carrot nose,
But where'd it go? A mystery grows!
Did someone eat it, say it ain't so,
Guess we'll just use a snowball, and go!

In this blizzard, we find our muse,
Warm hearts surround us, we cannot lose.
With jokes and laughter in snowy delight,
We'll tumble and roll until morning light!

Crystal Conundrum

The snowflakes dance like crazy bees,
While I attempt to catch them with ease.
They slip right past, a fluffy parade,
Leaving me laughing at my own charade.

With boots on backwards and mitten mismatched,
I tumble and fall, my dignity hatched.
I roll like a snowball, round and round,
In a winter wonderland, lost and found.

My dog barks frantically, snow in his snout,
Chasing the flakes, he's got it all out.
I join the frolic, a whimsical race,
As snow drifts pile up, a soft, white embrace.

The world is a canvas, painted in white,
With giggles and giggles, oh what a sight!
We build a snowman, a comedy queen,
With a carrot nose, the silliest seen.

A Portrait in Powder

Snow's artistic touch cloaks the dull ground,
Transforming the world without making a sound.
My neighbor's garden, a fluffy delight,
With gnomes wearing hats; what a curious sight!

The snowman's got style, a scarf that's too long,
It's flailing about, he's dancing along.
His buttons are buttons from an old coat,
And now he looks like a bad fashion note!

A cat peers out, on the window snug tight,
Judging our antics in pure feline fright.
With paws on the glass, she rolls her green eyes,
As we tumble and leap in our snowy disguise.

The snowball fight starts, and I let one fly,
It misses my target and lands in the sky!
Like a ninja on a mission, I dodge and weave,
But snow's not my ally, it's hard to believe!

Sunlit Snowflakes

Oh look! The sun's got its shades on today,
Mixing up winter with spring in a play.
The snow glimmers bright like a disco ball,
While I twirl in my boots, I'm ready to fall.

The kids are out howling, making a mess,
Their laughter a melody, some odd kind of stress.
"Snow angels!" they cry, in the fluff that surrounds,
While I watch my efforts come crashing down sounds.

As I make my way through the glistening fluff,
A wayward snowflake shouts, "Hey! That's tough!"
It lands on my nose, and I jump with surprise,
Then slip on an ice patch, oh what a demise!

Winter's a jester, with blizzards to boast,
Yet we toast to the snow, with laughter, we roast.
With cocoa in hand and hats on our heads,
We revel in chaos, surrounded by beds.

The Cold Within

Inside my house, the heater's on blast,
While outside my window, snow falls so fast.
With a mug full of cocoa, I grin with a cheer,
As icicles form like they have special smear.

The dog has snuggled right into my lap,
While I start to think, maybe it's a trap.
For every time I think I'm so cozy and fine,
Someone throws a snowball, I'm wet like a brine!

My friends all decide to drop in for a peek,
Dressed up in layers, they all look so chic.
We share our disaster stories of snow,
And laugh at the times we slipped after a throw.

With chuckles and giggles, the night tumbles on,
We toast to warm memories until they are gone.
So here's to the chill, and the chaos it brings,
With laughter and friendship, winter's heart sings.

Blanket of White

Puffy flakes dance from the sky,
Waking my neighbors with a sigh.
Children giggle, snowballs fly,
While I trip, oh my, oh my!

Sleds zoom down with a joyful cheer,
But I'm stuck, it's crystal clear.
I thought I'd glide, but here I am,
Building a snowman—just a sham!

Dogs dive in for a snowy spree,
While I sip cocoa, feeling glee.
Snowflakes land on my nose, oh dear,
Not sure if it's fun or sheer fear!

As the sun peeks out, I start to grin,
Shoveling paths with a determined chin.
I'll conquer this winter, come what may,
For tomorrow's mischief, I'll be ready to play!

Storm's Silent Scream

Whirls of white swirl with a twist,
I can't find my gloves—oh, what a list!
Is that a snowman or just a mound?
It's hard to say; I can't make a sound.

My cat's in a coat, looking quite spry,
He darts and slips, oh my, oh my!
He leaps with gusto, pretends he's a rabbit,
While I laugh, thinking he might just nab it!

The wind really howls, like a banshee in fright,
I'm clutching my coffee, oh what a sight!
Snow boots squelch in puddles and heaps,
While neighbors ponder winter's funny leaps.

Twirls of snowflakes fall all around,
I'm stuck in this blizzard—can't find solid ground.
But give me some cocoa and a map of the town,
I'll navigate snowdrifts with a goofy crown!

The Softest Plunge

With a plunk and a thud, I plunge in the snow,
Rolling about, feeling the glow.
It's a blizzard party, that's quite a tease,
Dancing snow angels with elegant ease.

My scarf is a squiggle, my hat's on my ear,
As I tumble and giggle, it's all so clear.
The snow's quite whispery, soft as a dream,
But my nose is red—oops, how extreme!

Winter's mischief brings frosty joy,
Snowflakes are gifts, like a glittering toy.
So come on, dear friends, let's play without care,
We'll bubble and bounce, going everywhere!

Dodge the snowballs and crafts full of cheer,
While I slip on ice—oh, the end is near!
But laughter is magic; warmth in our hearts,
In this wondrous winter, we'll play all our parts!

Crystal Confessions

The snow is whispering secrets so bright,
As I dress like a marshmallow, what a sight!
Waddling carefully, like a duck in a pond,
I spill my cocoa—it's truly beyond!

Snowflakes speak softly, but who's keeping score?
They never listen; just cover the floor.
I'll blame it on winter when dinner goes wrong,
"Sorry, my dear, it's just winter's song!"

The squirrels are plotting, I swear they conspire,
Rolling in snow as if they're on fire.
While I chase my hat, round and round we go,
The wind gives a giggle; it's just a show!

So gather, dear friends, and embrace this delight,
With each crystal flake, there's magic tonight.
In this frosty chaos, let laughter unite,
For winter's wild stories, we'll share with delight!

Echoes of Winter's Breath

Snowflakes twirl, a dance so bright,
While squirrels in jackets take flight.
A snowball fight, oh what a sight,
But my nose is red, it's quite a fright.

Snowmen giggle with button eyes,
While the dog stumbles, oh what a surprise!
"I'm just a pup!" he seems to shout,
In this fluffy world, there's never a doubt.

Hot cocoa wishes with marshmallow dreams,
Mittens that vanish in snowdrift themes.
Ice skating penguins slip and crash,
What a show, oh what a splash!

So let the winds blow and the flakes soar,
As laughter echoes, who could want more?
With winter's breath, we'll jest and play,
In this frosty fun, we'll stay all day.

The Artistry of Icicles

Icicles dangle, like lollipops pure,
Dripping from eaves, their beauty is sure.
But one little jab leaves me in dread,
"Oops," I declare, with a thump to my head!

Snowmen wear scarves that trail the floor,
While penguins in mittens run for the door.
Their waddles and flops bring giggles galore,
As we roll in the snow, hearts ready to soar.

The snow on the roof makes quite the sound,
It shakes and it rattles, then tumbles around.
Caught in this weather, we giggle and scream,
As we chase after snowflakes, a frosty daydream.

So grab your gear, let's tumble and twirl,
In a wintry realm where laughter does whirl.
With art made of ice, our spirits so high,
In this frozen delight, we'll never run dry.

Whispers Beneath the White Canopy

Beneath the white canopy, secrets are shared,
While snowflakes whisper, the world feels unpaired.
A blizzard of giggles spills from our lips,
As we tumble and tumble, our laughter now flips.

The cat in a coat looks very confused,
While kids in the snow are happily bruised.
With snowball missiles flying through the air,
Even the cold wind cannot stop our flair!

Mittens and boots create quite the fashion,
As we skateboard on snow, fueled by our passion.
Icicles dangle with a cheeky little grin,
As we carve out a penguin, let the chaos begin!

So dance in the snow, let your worries all flee,
In this wintry madness, we're wild and we're free.
With whispers of joy and frosty delight,
We'll conquer the snow till the day turns to night.

Melodies of the Snowbound Path

Up and down the snowbound trail,
Sleds are flying, we're sure to prevail.
Shouts of laughter blend with the chill,
As we zoom past trees with a snow-laden thrill.

A snowball war ignites with a bang,
While the squirrel looks on and lets out a clang.
I slip on a patch that makes me sway,
As snow drifts cloud, oh what a display!

Under the silhouettes of frosted pines,
We build our kingdom, where joy intertwines.
The beauty of winter unfolds as we sing,
Like a symphony played by the world's icy King.

With snowflakes as notes, our chorus does ring,
In this whisking weather where memories cling.
So let's jiggle and giggle, let our hearts part,
In these melodies of frost, we find our warm heart.

The Enigma of the Frosted Dawn

Morning light, a glimmer bright,
Blankets white, a comical sight.
Snowflakes dance, a clumsy show,
Chasing squirrels, dodging woe.

Coffee cups steam, noses red,
Snowmen laugh at what's been said.
With every step, slips and spins,
Winter's games and playful grins.

Boots are heavy, hearts are light,
Frosty bites and cheer take flight.
Giggles echo through the trees,
Cold cheeks warm with chilly breeze.

In this wonder, we frolic free,
Each snowball fight a jubilee.
Laughter rings, as cold winds blow,
In frosted realms, our joy will grow.

Trapped in the Winter's Lullaby

Snowflakes swirl, in dreamy cheer,
Sleds zoom past, too quick, oh dear!
With cheeks aglow and hats askew,
We conquer hills, a daring crew.

Mittens lost, a silly chase,
Snowmen frown with frosty grace.
Carrot noses, eyes of coal,
A frozen friend, that's our goal.

Winter's breath, a whisper low,
Funny tales with every throw.
As we tumble, laughter bursts,
In snowy worlds, our hearts immerse.

Hot cocoa sips, marshmallows afloat,
Chasing dreams on a fluffy boat.
Lullabies sung by winds so light,
Winter's grip, a funny delight.

Chill in the Air

Chill winds waft, a frosty tease,
Noses scrunch, oh, if you please!
Snowflakes tickle, a playful fight,
Hot cocoa dreams, in pure delight.

Sledding down the icy hill,
Laughter echoes, a joyful thrill.
With every tumble, giggles reign,
In this chill, we find no pain.

The snowman winks, a crafty grin,
Wearing mittens, he's all in.
Icicles dangle, a speckled crown,
Winter's antics never frown.

In cozy nooks, we snuggle tight,
With tales of joy that spark delight.
The chill outside, it can't compare,
To warmth within, with love to share.

Whispers of Winter's Wrath

Whispers soft, through trees they weave,
Tickling noses, as we believe.
Snowdrifts rise, a fortress tall,
In winter's grasp, we dream and sprawl.

Chilly breezes, a playful hum,
Sipping soup, our hearts go thrum.
Snowball fights with gleeful shouts,
In this chill, there's joy around.

Frosty breath, we race and dash,
Every snowflake, a gleeful splash.
As laughter rises, spirits soar,
In chilly climes, we ask for more.

Under skies of cloudy gray,
Every moment turns to play.
Winter's whispers, oh what legions,
In the cold, we find new reasons.

Epiphany in White

Snowflakes dance like silly fools,
Slipping on the ice, breaking rules.
Snowmen grin with carrot noses,
While kids fall down, a comical poses.

Hot cocoa spills in my warm embrace,
As snowballs fly, a chilly race.
Winter hats pulled over ears,
Laughing echoes, all the cheers.

The dog darts out, chasing that flake,
Tripping over its own silly shake.
With each fall, we find delight,
In our snow-filled, frosty fight.

So gather round, let's make it clear,
This winter's joy brings everyone near.
With laughter shared and frostbite woes,
We celebrate the snowstorm's throes.

The Howling Silence

Whispers of snow in the still night,
A husky dashes, what a sight!
His owner slips, oh what a fall,
What's that? Just echoes, not a call.

Icicles hang like toothy grins,
As penguins waddle, oh where to begin?
They slide by like some slick-o soap,
While we stand by, just gaping, nope!

Inside, we hide with tea in hand,
Wishing for sun on this frozen land.
But with each flake, the giggles grow,
In cozy corners, warmth in tow.

For even in silence, winter's charm,
Brings laughter shared, a joyful balm.
With furry friends all bundled tight,
We'll laugh until it's morning light.

Tides of Ice

A wave of snow crashes on the shore,
With every drift, we giggle more.
Sleds on hills, a swirling spree,
The sea of white is laughing, whee!

Snow angels spread their frosty wings,
As laughter lifts, the heart just sings.
A penguin parade, what a sight,
Marching forward, oh what a fright!

Hats blown off by the swirling gusts,
In this blizzard, it's all just trust.
We bundle up, for now, we'll stay,
In winter's grasp, we find our play.

For even as the cold winds howl,
In every flake, we dance and prowl.
With friends beside, the world does glow,
As we sculpt memories in the snow.

Invisibility of the Storm

Where has the world gone, buried wide?
Beneath the fluff, surprise and slide!
What once was grass, now fluff and fun,
In every flake, a race begun.

Sneaky snowmen come to life,
With hats and scarves, what a strife!
Each twig a weapon, winter's fight,
Snowballs fly like stars at night.

We lose our ways, I trip and tumble,
In this great freeze, who can be humble?
The dog leaps high, a snowy dive,
In this chaotic world, we thrive.

So gather round, let's dance and cheer,
In the storm, we shed our fear.
For winter's whimsy, laughter shared,
Turns invisible storms to joy declared.

Tempest's Track

Chill winds giggle, snowflakes waltz,
They dance around, like playful pals.
A snowman stumbles, hat goes askew,
Laughing so hard, we fall—who knew?

Hot cocoa spills, we jump and shout,
In fuzzy socks, we twist about.
The dog leaps high, bites at the air,
While we slide down on winter's chair.

Squirrels wear mittens, what a sight!
Building snow forts, ready for fright.
The snowball flies, we duck and dive,
In this chilled world, we're so alive!

As the sun peeks through icy lace,
We giggle and run, a cheerful chase.
In this frosty fun, we find our groove,
Snowy shenanigans, we just can't lose!

Dreams in the Drifts

Pillows of snow, oh, what a thrill!
We jump and sink, our hearts to fill.
With each surprise, laughter erupts,
In winter's game, it's joy disrupted.

Snowflakes tickle, noses turn red,
Falling down soft, we bounce instead.
A mitten lost, a hat in flight,
Who knew snow day could be this bright?

Snow angels giggle beneath the skies,
Imagining wings, we try to rise.
A slip and a slide, a tumble so loud,
Winter's wildness draws a huge crowd.

In this frosty dream, we're young and bold,
Finding warm laughter in the cold.
With every cheer, the world feels right,
Snow-drenched happiness, oh, what a sight!

Stars Captured in Snow

Twinkling lights hide in white fluff,
We chase every glitter, is this enough?
The moon winks down, plays peekaboo,
With laughter so bright, we shimmy and pursue.

Snowflakes wear wigs, a fashion spree,
Snowman catwalks beneath the tree.
We can't help but snicker at each slip,
Joy in our hearts, they can't take that trip.

Beneath the stars, we spin and glide,
In this winter wonderland, our dreams collide.
A snowball toss and a giggly retreat,
The chilly night can't knock off our beat.

Chasing the glimmers, the sparkles so bright,
Each snowball thrown, a dazzling flight.
In this frosty tale, we feel the glow,
As we dance with stars caught in the snow!

Cold Caresses

A sudden chill, cheeks turn to pink,
The snowflakes swirl, quicker than you think.
With every gust, the laughter lifts high,
We ski on dreams, under the low sky.

The dog's on a mission, burrowing deep,
While we spin round like toys, in a heap.
A snow-covered wand, we're wizards today,
Casting giggles and fun in a frosty display.

The sleigh bells jingle, we gather 'round,
Making memories in this magic town.
With sleds racing fast, we hug the slides,
In this winter world, joy surely abides.

As the night casts its velvet cloak,
With winked eyes, we whisper and joke.
For in the cold's soft, tender embrace,
Is where we find our most cherished place!

Surrender to the Chill

When snowflakes dance like silly sprites,
My toes feel cold on winter nights.
The wind it howls, a joker's song,
Yet here I am, where I belong.

With mittens lost, I'm on the run,
Building snowmen, oh what fun!
My scarf's a mess, like spaghetti twirled,
In this frosty, wacky world.

Snowballs flying, laughter high,
Mom says, 'Don't play, you might cry!'
But look at me all bundled tight,
A snowball warrior in the night!

So here I stand, in layers grand,
Giggling at my frozen hand.
With every slip, I craft my tale,
Winter's whimsy won't derail!

Sleet Singing Softly

The sleet it dances, such a tease,
It tickles noses, brings me to my knees!
I slip and slide like a clumsy seal,
While hot cocoa calls, a warm appeal.

My hat is crooked, my boots askew,
I look like art, not quite brand new.
But in this mess, I laugh and shout,
'Who needs a car? I'll just slip about!'

The trees are coated, glistening bright,
Like a cake topped with sugary light.
I toss a snowball, oh what a throw,
With laughter ringing wherever I go!

So let it sleet, let it fall,
I'll take a tumble and stand tall.
With every cold, absurd delight,
I'll sing my song through winter night!

The Lullaby of the North

Under a blanket of silvery white,
The world's asleep, a sleepy sight.
But wait! A squirrel with acorn stash,
Chasing snowflakes with a clumsy dash.

The stars above, like glitter spills,
Watch the antics, the snowy thrills.
While snowmen nodding in quiet glee,
Exchange some secrets with the trees.

Then comes the plow, a rumbly king,
And children cheer, their joyous ring.
We build a fort, our castle grand,
Defending our realm with snowball in hand.

With giggles echoing through the chill,
Night wraps us tight, but you know the thrill.
In frosty hugs, winter's embrace,
A lullaby of laughter in this icy space!

Frost and Fire

The chill outside, it bites and gnaws,
But in the kitchen, I'm the boss!
With cookies baking, warmth and spice,
I'll conquer winter, oh so nice.

The snowflakes tumble, what a show,
Each one a dancer, what's the flow?
While socks are damp and hair a frizz,
I'm shaking off that winter fizz!

The fireplace crackles with a grin,
As hot cocoa gets a frosty spin.
With every sip, I'm full of cheer,
Even the snowmen laugh and leer.

So bring on the frost, I'm not afraid,
I'll dance and laugh in this snowy glade.
With warmth inside, I raise my cup,
To winter fuzzies, let's warm up!

Milton Keynes UK
Ingram Content Group UK Ltd.
UKHW021938121124
451129UK00007B/131